PUFFIN BOOKS

RAIDING AND TRADING:
VIKINGS WITH A FEW GORY BITS

Scoular Anderson studied graphic design at the Glasgow School of Art. He then worked as an illustrator for London University and as a teacher in a large comprehensive school in central Scotland. He began illustrating and writing both for children and adults after leaving art school. He now lives in his native Argyllshire in the west of Scotland, where he works freelance.

GW00373834

Scoular Anderson

Raiding and Trading:

Vikings With a Few Gory Bits

PUFFIN BOOKS

PUFFIN BOOKS

Published by the Penguin Group
Penguin Books Ltd, 27 Wrights Lane, London W8 5TZ, England
Penguin Putnam Inc., 375 Hudson Street, New York, New York 10014, USA
Penguin Books Australia Ltd, Ringwood, Victoria, Australia
Penguin Books Canada Ltd, 10 Alcorn Avenue, Toronto, Ontario, Canada M4V 3B2
Penguin Books (NZ) Ltd, 182–190 Wairau Road, Auckland 10, New Zealand

Penguin Books Ltd, Registered Offices: Harmondsworth, Middlesex, England

First published 1998
1 3 5 7 9 10 8 6 4 2

Typeset in Bembo

Made and printed in England by Clays Ltd, St Ives plc

British Library Cataloguing in Publication Data
A CIP catalogue record for this book is available from the British Library

ISBN 0–140–38474–X

CONTENTS

WHO WERE THE VIKINGS?

The Vikings have a bad reputation. They are usually thought of as cruel thugs who sailed from home in their ships to plunder and kill in other lands.

This was partly true. The things a Viking most admired were skill at fighting, courage in battle and success and adventure on expeditions.

However, plundering and killing were quite common in those times. Lots of other peoples did the same thing.

1

The Vikings had a peaceful side to their lives, too. They were good farmers and skilled craftsmen. They were busy traders who sailed vast distances to sell their wares. They were eager explorers, keen to find out what lay at the end of a river or beyond the seas. They even reached America long before Christopher Columbus.

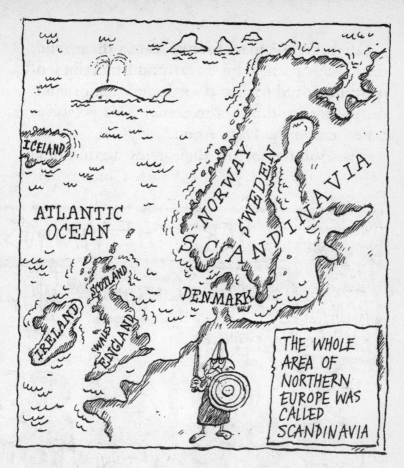

The Vikings came from the northern parts of Europe. They lived there in communities of farms, villages and towns ruled over by chieftains.

Slowly these communities joined together and became the countries of Norway, Sweden and Denmark that we know today. Each country had a king.

After the Roman Empire came to an end, Europe was in a bit of a muddle. Tribes of people moved back and forth looking for lands to plunder and places to settle. This period is often called the Dark Ages.

The Vikings began their raids at this time

WHERE THE VIKINGS

THE DARK AGES

VIKINGS

THE MIDDLE AGES

ROMAN EMPIRE

HUNS, AVARS, FRANKS, SAXONS, GOTHS, ANGLES, ETC. ETC. ETC.

ABOUT AD 500

ABOUT 800

ABOUT 1100

and they terrorized the people of Europe for about three hundred years.

The raids stopped when other people at last managed to gather armies strong enough to fend off the Vikings.

The Vikings then settled down to a more peaceful life.

FIT IN HISTORY

TUDORS AND STUARTS | 18TH CENTURY | 19TH CENTURY | 20TH CENTURY

1485   1714   1800   1900   2000

VIKING SHIPS

There was a good reason why the Vikings were successful raiders and traders – their ships.

The Vikings were skilful shipbuilders and superb sailors. They built many types of boats – cargo ships, small rowing boats and travel ships to take settlers to new lands.

Their most famous ships are the warships or longships. They were long, thin and light so they could be taken into shallow water. They could be pulled up on beaches or even carried overland.

They were flexible so they would bend in stormy seas. They sailed swiftly over the surface of the water using a single sail. Oars were used when there was no wind or the ship was close to shore.

THE VIKINGS WERE VERY PROUD OF THEIR SHIPS. THEY WERE GIVEN NAMES LIKE *LONGSERPENT*, *DRAGON* OR *WAVESTRIDER*. THE SHIPS WERE OFTEN MENTIONED IN VIKING POEMS.

The Vikings had no navigation instrument. They had to rely on their knowledge of the sea to guide their ships – especially if the land was out of sight.

NAVIGATION AIDS

* THE POSITIONS OF THE SUN, MOON AND STARS IN THE SKY.

* TIDES, CURRENTS AND WEATHER CONDITIONS.

* COUNTING THE DAYS SINCE LEAVING PORT.

* FLOATING ICE. (TOO FAR NORTH!)

* SEA MAMMALS AND BIRDS. (SOME BIRDS ALWAYS FLY TO LAND TO ROOST AT NIGHT.)

* FISH. (SOME FISH GATHER IN CERTAIN PARTS OF THE SEA.)

* SMELL! (THE SMELL OF SHEEP WHEN CLOSE TO LAND, FOR INSTANCE.)

I can smell camels.

WOW! We're well off course!

THE VIKING LONG-SHIP

THE VIKINGS BUILT THEIR SHIPS WITHOUT PLANS. THEY USED SIMPLE TOOLS.

TONGS

HAMMER

ADZE

AXE

HOLE BORER

KNIFE

SAW

STERN

TILLER

STEERING OAR

HOLES OR PORTS FOR THE OARS.

THE PORTS HAD COVERS TO CLOSE THE HOLES AND STOP WATER GETTING INTO THE SHIP WHILE UNDER SAIL.

8

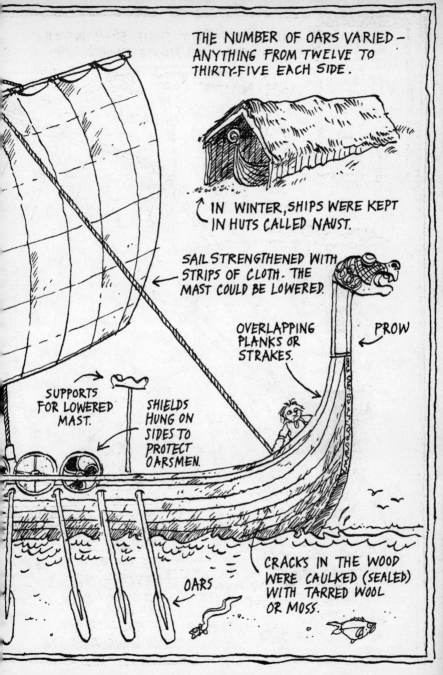

THE NUMBER OF OARS VARIED — ANYTHING FROM TWELVE TO THIRTY-FIVE EACH SIDE.

IN WINTER, SHIPS WERE KEPT IN HUTS CALLED NAUST.

SAIL STRENGTHENED WITH STRIPS OF CLOTH. THE MAST COULD BE LOWERED.

OVERLAPPING PLANKS OR STRAKES.

PROW

SUPPORTS FOR LOWERED MAST.

SHIELDS HUNG ON SIDES TO PROTECT OARSMEN.

OARS

CRACKS IN THE WOOD WERE CAULKED (SEALED) WITH TARRED WOOL OR MOSS.

9

MORE SHIP FACTS

THERE WERE NO SEATS IN THE SHIPS. OARSMEN SAT ON CHESTS WHICH CONTAINED THEIR BELONGINGS.

I don't care if you've got a snuffly nose. You can't look for your handkerchief now!

ANCHORS WERE MADE OF IRON OR STONES IN A WOODEN FRAME.

THERE WAS A DEEP AREA IN THE MIDDLE OF THE SHIP WHERE CARGO WAS STORED.

THE VIKINGS BUILT CANALS. SOMETIMES THEY WERE BUILT AS SHORT CUTS BETWEEN TWO SEAS. SOME CANALS WERE BUILT SO THAT SHIPS COULD BE TAKEN TO A CALM INLAND LAKE FOR PROTECTION.

THE SHIPS WERE LIGHT ENOUGH TO BE CARRIED ROUND OBSTACLES IN RIVERS OR ACROSS NARROW LAND BETWEEN TWO STRETCHES OF WATER.

THE KNARRS WERE VIKING CARGO SHIPS. THEY WERE MUCH BROADER AND DEEPER THAN THE LONGSHIPS. ALTHOUGH THEY HAD A FEW OAR PORTS THEY WERE REALLY SAILING SHIPS. VIKINGS USED THESE SHIPS TO CARRY THEIR FAMILIES, BELONGINGS AND ANIMALS TO NEW SETTLEMENTS. THERE ARE PLACES IN ICELAND CALLED KNARRARNES AND KNARRARSUND WHICH HAVE BEEN NAMED AFTER THESE BOATS.

IF THERE WAS NO HARBOUR, CARGO WOULD HAVE BEEN TAKEN OFF BY ROWING BOAT.

11

SCANDINAVIA

• NOVGOROD

THE PEOPLE WHO LIVED
IN THIS AREA WERE SLAVS.
THEY CALLED THE VIKINGS
RUS. SO MANY VIKINGS
CAME TO THIS LAND THAT
IT EVENTUALLY BECAME
KNOWN AS *RUSSIA*.

THE VIKINGS
FOUNDED THE
TRADING CITIES
OF NOVGOROD
AND KIEV.

ROUTE
FROM
FAR EAST.

VIKINGS
TRAVELLED
ON RUSSIAN
RIVERS.

KIEV

CASPIAN
SEA

P E

BLACK SEA

BYZANTIUM

THERE WERE SO MANY
VIKING TRADERS IN THE
CITY OF BYZANTIUM
THAT PART OF THE
CITY WAS KNOWN AS
THE 'VIKING QUARTER'.

MEDITERRANEAN SEA

TRADE AND TRAVEL

The Vikings travelled great distances to trade and explore. They were away from home for long periods of time and faced all sorts of hardships and dangers. They obviously thought it was worth the trouble and they were able to return home with their ships full of exotic goods.

WHAT THE VIKINGS HAD ON OFFER:

- WALRUS IVORY (FOR CARVING)
- ANIMAL SKINS
- FURS
- AMBER (FOSSILIZED RESIN OF TREES—FOR BEADS, JEWELLERY ETC.)
- ROPES OF WALRUS HIDE
- FEATHERS (FOR PILLOWS, QUILTS)
- WHETSTONES (FOR SHARPENING KNIVES ETC.)
- SOAPSTONE COOKING POTS
- SLAVES

I've a complaint about this amber I bought from you last year...

They brought home silks, spices, silver, wine, fine jewellery, glassware and pottery.

The Vikings didn't use money but instead exchanged goods with other merchants.

Sometimes they used silver to pay for things. This was usually pieces of silver cut from jewellery or foreign coins.

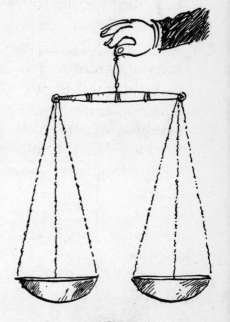

THE TRADERS CARRIED WITH THEM LITTLE COLLAPSIBLE WEIGHING-SCALES TO WEIGH THE CORRECT AMOUNT OF SILVER.

BOX FOR SCALES

The Vikings crossed Europe by seas, lakes, and rivers. They travelled either in small groups of people in one boat or in huge fleets of dozens of ships.

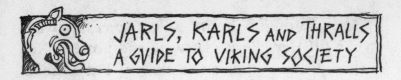

JARLS, KARLS AND THRALLS
A GUIDE TO VIKING SOCIETY

Viking society was divided into four groups.

KINGS

Scandinavia was made up of many small kingdoms. Their borders were always changing as some kingdoms grew larger and others got smaller.

Kings were expected to lead their warriors into battle and protect the people in their kingdom.

When a king died his eldest son did not always become the new king. Someone else in the royal family could be chosen.

JARLS

Jarls were wealthy and powerful. They were chieftains who owned lands at home and led their warriors abroad on raiding expeditions.

These local chieftains were very powerful. If their king became unpopular they could have him killed or exiled.

CHILDHOOD WAS SHORT IN VIKING TIMES. CHILDREN WERE EXPECTED TO HELP THEIR PARENTS AT THEIR WORK FROM AN EARLY AGE. GIRLS WOULD HELP THEIR MOTHERS IN THE HOUSE. BOYS WOULD HELP ON THE FARM. SOME BOYS WENT RAIDING WHEN THEY WERE TEENAGERS.

Just keep clear of their blades...

KARLS

Karls were free men and women. Many had their own farms and were quite wealthy. Others were servants, farm-workers or hunters.

A farmer's eldest son inherited his land so younger sons usually became warriors, merchants or craftsmen.

A VIKING WOMAN HAD MANY DUTIES. APART FROM RUNNING THE HOUSE, SHE WOULD BREW BEER AND WEAVE CLOTH FOR CLOTHES. SHE WOULD TEND PEOPLE WHO WERE SICK AND KNEW HOW TO MIX REMEDIES FROM HERBS.

If you don't drink this cough medicine you won't be allowed to watch the wrestling.

Aw, yuk!

THRALLS

Thralls were slaves. Criminals were sometimes punished by being made slaves but most slaves were captured during raids.

Slaves worked in houses or on the land. They were bought and sold like goods. They had no rights, though some hard-working slaves could earn their freedom.

THE WIFE USUALLY LOOKED AFTER THE KEYS OF HER HUSBAND'S STRONGBOX WHERE VALUABLES WERE STORED. SHE WOULD RUN THE FARM WHEN HE WAS AWAY RAIDING OR TRADING. IT'S THOUGHT THAT SOME WOMEN DID MEN'S JOBS, LIKE BEING A MERCHANT, A RUNE-CARVER OR SKALD (POET).

THINGS, TRIALS and HONOUR

The King was his people's leader. He was expected to protect them and bring them honour but he didn't make laws. The laws were made by the Thing.

The Thing was a sort of parliament. Because people lived in widely-scattered farms and villages, the Thing took place only once or twice a year. It was held in the open air at a special place like a field or hillside.

Freemen would spend about a week at their local Thing discussing many problems. Nothing was written down so decisions and new laws had to be memorized by officials.

The Thing was also a bit like a fair. Tents and kitchens were set up. Merchants came and set up their stalls. It was a chance for friends and relatives to meet each other and catch up with the gossip.

Family ties were very important. People were expected to be loyal to their family and uphold its honour. (The family could be as big as a tribe as it included uncles, aunts, cousins and distant relatives.)

If someone received an insult, his family would seek revenge. Sometimes feuds between families lasted for years or even generations and there would be much bloodshed.

SOME ARGUMENTS WERE SETTLED BY A DUEL. THE TWO DUELLISTS HAD TO KEEP WITHIN A SQUARE MARKED BY POSTS OR A PIECE OF CLOTH.

People suspected of a crime were put on trial at the Thing. If it was difficult to tell if they were guilty or innocent, the accused were given some tests . . .

WOMEN HAD TO PICK STONES FROM A CAULDRON OF BOILING WATER. MEN HAD TO CARRY RED-HOT IRON A FEW PACES.

IF THEY DROPPED THE STONE OR IRON THEY WERE CONSIDERED GUILTY. IF THEY COMPLETED THE TASK, THEIR WOUNDS WERE INSPECTED AFTER A WEEK. IF THEY WERE HEALING WELL THEY WERE CONSIDERED INNOCENT.

Aieeee!

Urk!

GUILTY!

Guilty people could be fined, made slaves or exiled.

VIKING CLOTHES

The Vikings took great care of their appearance. We know they had ear scoops for cleaning their ears, tweezers, toothpicks and washing bowls.

The wealthy were well dressed and well groomed but the slaves wore ragged clothes. Viking raiders didn't have much time to keep themselves smart. Strangers often described them as being 'filthy and unwashed'.

All sorts of jewellery and fine cloth were brought home by raiders and traders. The Vikings were probably quite fashionable for their times. Their clothes were dyed in many colours and decorated and trimmed with fur, embroidery and fine metalwork.

WOMEN WORE LONG DRESSES. THEY WERE USUALLY
COVERED BY A TUNIC HELD IN PLACE AT THE SHOULDERS
BY DECORATIVE BROOCHES.

HEAD-
SCARF →

CHAINS WITH USEFUL THINGS LIKE
SCISSORS, NEEDLE CASE, KNIFE,
KEYS ETC.

A RICH LADY WITH A SHAWL,
JEWELLERY AND A DRESS WITH
A LONG TRAIN. HER HAIR IS
WOVEN INTO A FANCY STYLE.

MEN WORE VARIOUS KINDS OF TROUSERS.

THE BAGGY LOOK

THE TIGHT LOOK

THE FLARED LOOK

THE SHORT LOOK

SHORT LEATHER BOOTS OR SHOES WERE FASTENED WITH LACES OR TOGGLES MADE OF ANTLER HORN.

CHILDREN WORE THE SAME KIND OF CLOTHES AS ADULTS.

CLOTH OR WOOL CAP.

A FARMER WEARING A SIMPLE TUNIC.

WOOLLEN TROUSERS.

A MERCHANT DRESSED FOR COLD WEATHER.

HE WEARS SEVERAL LAYERS OF CLOTHES, A HEAVY CLOAK AND A FUR HAT.

A RICH MAN WITH A WOOLLEN CLOAK. HIS CLOTHES ARE RICHLY EMBROIDERED AND HIS BELT HAS SILVER BUCKLES.

HAIRSTYLES

Both men and women wore their hair long. They liked to tie and braid their hair in different styles.

MEN USUALLY HAD BEARDS.

THEY BRAIDED THEIR HAIR AND BEARDS OR WORE HEADBANDS TO KEEP THE HAIR OUT OF THEIR EYES.

WOMEN GREW THEIR HAIR LONG.

IT WAS USUALLY TIED UP IN A FANCY TOP-KNOT.

AFTER MARRIAGE, WOMEN COVERED THEIR HAIR WITH A SCARF OR CAP.

WARRIORS

The Viking warriors believed that glory and bravery in battle were the most important things in life. They were always ready to fight when ordered to by their king or chieftain. Many Viking warriors became mercenaries (hired soldiers). There were plenty of foreign rulers who were eager to employ fighters with such a fierce reputation.

VIKING SWORDS WERE TREASURED BY THEIR OWNERS AND OFTEN HANDED DOWN FROM FATHER TO SON. THEY WERE COSTLY ITEMS BUT USUALLY BEAUTIFULLY DECORATED. THEIR OWNERS GAVE THEM NAMES LIKE:

MAIL-BITER
GOLDEN HILT
FIERCE
ADDER
LEG-BITER

A FULLER, WHICH IS A GROOVE IN THE BLADE MAKING IT LIGHTER AND MORE FLEXIBLE.

DOUBLE-EDGED.

← BATTLEAXE.

HELMET WITH
EYE-PROTECTORS.

WOODEN SHIELD
EDGED WITH METAL.
METAL CENTRE
PROTECTS HAND.

SPE[

CHAIN-
MAIL
TUNIC.

PADDED
JACKET.

CLOAK FASTENED AT THE
RIGHT TO ALLOW FREE
MOVEMENT OF SWORD ARM.

ARCHER
WITH BOW
AND
QUIVER.

LONG CHAIN-MAIL
COAT (SPLIT FOR
HORSE RIDING).

Before battles, leaders would make rousing speeches to their men. Then the two armies would shout abuse at each other, roar battle cries and rattle their weapons. Sometimes stones were thrown before the real battle began.

SOME WARRIORS WERE KNOWN AS BERSERKERS (THOUGHT TO BE FROM THE WORD BEAR-SARK OR BEARSKIN TUNIC). THEY WORKED THEMSELVES UP INTO A REAL FIGHTING FRENZY BEFORE BATTLE BY YELLING AND BITING THE EDGES OF THEIR SHIELDS.

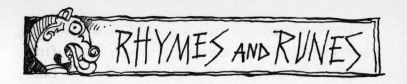

RHYMES AND RUNES

When a battle was won, the Vikings liked to record their victory. However, they didn't have ink, pens, or paper. Every fact had to be memorized and it was the job of the Skald (a kind of poet and record keeper) to do this.

Then, by the fireside on dark winter nights, the Skald would retell some of those stories to the chieftain and his family. The stories were handed down from father to son until they were written down by monks many centuries later.

...and when Brushwood Belly burst into the house, Bolli raised his sword called Leg-Biter and with one fearful stroke...

Long stories and poems were called sagas. These were often a family history as they recorded events like feuds, gory duels, marriages, births and adventurous expeditions.

The Vikings did write some things down, using writing called Runes. The letters were designed to be scratched on wood, stone or bone.

THE ALPHABET WAS CALLED *FUTHARK* AFTER THE FIRST SIX CHARACTERS, JUST AS WE SAY ABC.

ᚠ ᚢ ᚦ ᚨ ᚱ ᚲ

F U TH A R K

THE ALPHABET DIDN'T HAVE ANY CURVES (WHICH WERE DIFFICULT TO CARVE) OR HORIZONTAL LINES (WHICH MIGHT BE CONFUSED WITH THE GRAIN IN WOOD).

ᚼ ᚾ ᛁ ᛆ ᛋ

H N I A S

↑ ᛒ ᛘ ᛚ ᛦ

T B M L R

WORDS WERE CARVED ON THINGS LIKE COMBS, SHIPS AND SWORDS.

BILLS, LISTS AND LETTERS WERE CARVED AND SENT ON STICKS.

A LOVE LETTER HAS BEEN FOUND ON A PIECE OF BONE WHICH SIMPLY SAYS 'KISS ME'.

I wish Uncle Forktooth wouldn't send such long letters.

The Vikings decorated large stones with runes and pictures. These stones were then erected in a place where people could see them. Some of the stones celebrated bravery in battle, others praised good friends or were in remembrance of a dead relative.

A WEALTHY LANDOWNER CALLED JARLEBANKE BUILT A CAUSEWAY ACROSS SOME MARSHY GROUND. HE THEN HAD STONES ERECTED AT EACH END OF THE CAUSEWAY. THE WRITING ON THE STONES POINTED OUT TO TRAVELLERS WHO HAD BUILT THE CAUSEWAY.

Huh, show-off!

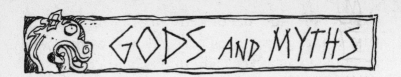

GODS AND MYTHS

The Vikings had a large number of colourful gods. People usually chose one god to worship or they might pray to different gods at different times – at the start of the harvest, for instance, or before going into battle.

There were no temples but people would go to worship in sacred places, often beside rivers or large rocks or in woods.

They made offerings to their gods. They took baskets of food to holy places, sprinkled bread on their fields or held noisy feasts.

Sometimes animals (and even humans) were sacrificed and hung on poles.

There were two families of gods – the Vanir who were gods of peace and plenty, and the Aesir who were gods of war.

Which one are we worshipping?

SOME OF THE AESIR

ODIN KING OF THE GODS. HE WAS MYSTERIOUS, WISE YET UNPREDICTABLE. HE LIVED IN A GREAT HALL CALLED *VALHALLA*, SURROUNDED BY WARRIORS WHO HAD BEEN KILLED IN BATTLE. THE BEAMS OF THE HALL WERE MADE OF SPEARS, THE ROOF-TILES WERE SHIELDS AND IT HAD 540 DOORS.

HUGIN AND MUNIN, ODIN'S RAVENS, FLEW AROUND THE WORLD, HEARING AND SEEING EVERYTHING.

GOLD HELMET

THE SPEAR GUGNIR, FORGED BY DWARFS, NEVER MISSED ITS MARK.

SLEIPNER, ODIN'S SWIFT, EIGHT-LEGGED HORSE.

ODIN COULD CHANGE SHAPE AND OFTEN WENT ROUND DISGUISED AS A HUMBLE TRAVELLER.

THOR

THOR WAS THE GOD OF STRENGTH, FIGHTING AND STORMS. HE CREATED THUNDER AND LIGHTNING AS HE RODE THROUGH THE SKIES. HE WAS THE MOST POPULAR GOD AND PEOPLE LIKED TO WEAR A REPLICA OF THOR'S HAMMER AROUND THEIR NECKS AS A GOOD-LUCK CHARM.

RED HAIR AND BUSHY BEARD.

THOR'S HAMMER MJOLNIR - THE DESTROYER.

IRON GLOVES.

THOR WAS CHEERFUL BUT A BIT STUPID, QUICK TO ANGER, YET QUICK TO CALM DOWN AGAIN.

HIS CHARIOT WAS PULLED BY TWO GOATS.

HE LIKED TO FIGHT GIANTS AND SERPENTS.

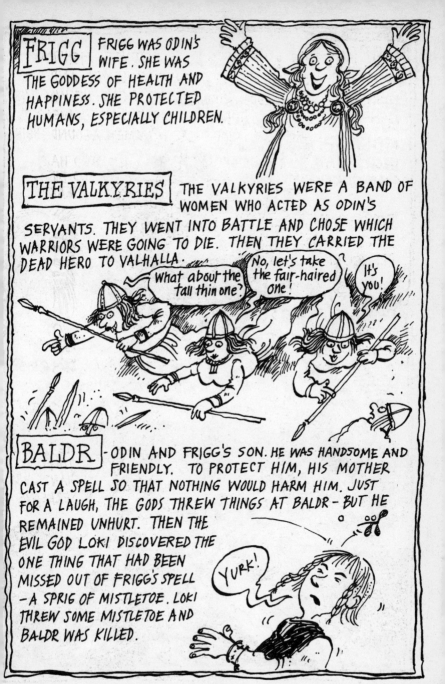

FRIGG FRIGG WAS ODIN'S WIFE. SHE WAS THE GODDESS OF HEALTH AND HAPPINESS. SHE PROTECTED HUMANS, ESPECIALLY CHILDREN.

THE VALKYRIES THE VALKYRIES WERE A BAND OF WOMEN WHO ACTED AS ODIN'S SERVANTS. THEY WENT INTO BATTLE AND CHOSE WHICH WARRIORS WERE GOING TO DIE. THEN THEY CARRIED THE DEAD HERO TO VALHALLA.

BALDR — ODIN AND FRIGG'S SON. HE WAS HANDSOME AND FRIENDLY. TO PROTECT HIM, HIS MOTHER CAST A SPELL SO THAT NOTHING WOULD HARM HIM. JUST FOR A LAUGH, THE GODS THREW THINGS AT BALDR — BUT HE REMAINED UNHURT. THEN THE EVIL GOD LOKI DISCOVERED THE ONE THING THAT HAD BEEN MISSED OUT OF FRIGG'S SPELL — A SPRIG OF MISTLETOE. LOKI THREW SOME MISTLETOE AND BALDR WAS KILLED.

39

SOME OF THE VANIR

FREY FREY WAS THE GOD OF SUNLIGHT AND RAIN, FORESTS AND FIELDS. HE WAS ALSO THE GOD OF FARMERS, MERCHANTS AND SAILORS.

FREY TRAVELLED IN A CHARIOT PULLED BY A GIANT BOAR, SWIFTER THAN A HORSE.
HE ALSO HAD A SHIP THAT COULD OUT-SAIL ANY OTHER. IT COULD BE FOLDED UP INTO A POCKET.

FREYA FREYA WAS FREY'S TWIN SISTER. SHE WAS THE GODDESS OF LOVE AND DEATH.

HER CHARIOT WAS PULLED BY TWO GIANT CATS.

SHE COULD SEE INTO THE FUTURE AND TRANSFORM HERSELF INTO DIFFERENT SHAPES.

THE VIKING UNIVERSE

THE VIKINGS IMAGINED THE UNIVERSE AS A PLACE WITH THREE LEVELS HELD TOGETHER BY A GIANT TREE.

STAGS NIBBLE THE SHOOTS OF THE TREE.

THE EVERGREEN ASH TREE CALLED YGGDRASIL WHOSE ROOTS HELD THE UNIVERSE TOGETHER

BEYOND THE SEA OF MIDGARD LIVE EVIL GIANTS AND DWARFS.

LEVEL ONE: ASGARD HOME OF THE GODS.

LEVEL TWO: MIDGARD HOME OF HUMANS.

SEA

JORMUNGAND THE SEA SERPENT WHICH SURROUNDS MIDGARD

LEVEL THREE NIFLHEIM AND MUSPELLHEIM, LANDS OF DARKNESS, FIRE AND ICE. HOME OF THE DEAD.

THE DRAGON NIDHOGG WHO CHEWS THE TREE ROOTS.

THE COMING OF CHRISTIANITY

Throughout the Viking age, the Vikings worshipped their own gods. But elsewhere in Europe, missionaries were travelling around, converting people to the Christian religion.

Many Viking raiders and traders came into contact with Christians on their travels. They may have been impressed by Christian churches and religious ceremonies. Some merchants wore crosses round their necks or became Christians because it helped their trade in Christian countries.

Finally, missionaries reached Scandinavia but they were not very successful at first. It took about two hundred years to convert all the Vikings to Christianity. The two religions lasted for a long time side by side.

VIKINGS WORE A LUCKY CHARM ROUND THEIR NECKS. IT WAS A MINIATURE REPLICA OF THE GOD THOR'S HAMMER. THE CHRISTIAN CROSS LOOKED VERY LIKE THE HAMMER.

CRAFTSMEN OFTEN HAD MOULDS WITH BOTH SHAPES ON THEM.

A STONE VIKING CROSS FROM YORKSHIRE. IT'S A MIXTURE OF CHRISTIAN CROSS AND TRADITIONAL VIKING CARVING. A WARRIOR IS SHOWN WITH HIS WEAPONS.

THIS WOODEN CHURCH (IN NORWAY) WAS BUILT AFTER THE VIKING AGE BUT IS DECORATED WITH VIKING DRAGONS.

VIKINGS AT HOME

Most Vikings were farmers who lived in farmsteads scattered throughout the country.

Their houses were built of either wood, stone, turf, or wattle and daub (clay, straw and sometimes dung, plastered over a framework of twigs). It depended on what materials were easiest to find. For the roofs they used thatch – strips of wood or grassy turf.

SOME HOUSES HAD ANGLED POSTS TO HELP SUPPORT THE ROOF.

A HOUSE OF STONE AND TURF.

BENCHES FOR SITTING OR SLEEPING ON.

Most farmhouses consisted of just one large hall where the family and servants lived and slept. In winter there would be a pen at one end for farm animals.

Some farmsteads had extra rooms – one for the chieftain, for instance, so he could have some privacy.

SMOKE FROM THE FIRE WENT OUT THROUGH A HOLE IN THE ROOF.

CUTAWAY VIEW OF A VIKING HOUSE.

THERE MIGHT HAVE BEEN ONE OR TWO SPECIAL PIECES OF FURNITURE LIKE A CHAIR WITH CARVED DECORATIONS.

45

A VIKING FARM

A SMALL FARM WOULD BE RUN BY THE
FARMER AND HIS FAMILY. WEALTHY
FARMERS EMPLOYED PEOPLE TO HELP ON
THE FARM OR USED SLAVES.
SOME MEN HAD SPECIAL TRADES, LIKE
THE BLACKSMITH OR COOPER (BARREL-MAKER).
THEY EITHER WORKED ON THE FARM OR
TRAVELLED ROUND THE COUNTRY.

THE VIKINGS
USED THE
KIND OF TOOLS
WE SEE TODAY:
RAKES, SPADES,
HOES, SICKLES
AND PLOUGH.

LONGHOUSE (MAIN HOME)

FOOD STORE. FISH AND MEAT WERE SALTED, DRIED OR SMOKED TO PROVIDE FOOD THROUGHOUT THE WINTER.

VEGETABLE GARDEN.

THE VIKING FARM ANIMALS:
COWS   PIGS
SHEEP   CHICKENS
GOATS   GEESE
HORSES

47

A lot of time must have been spent making cloth and clothes. Wool and flax (fibres from a plant) were spun into thread then woven into cloth on a loom.

Women embroidered strips of complicated, colourful designs to trim clothes with. They also made tapestries to hang on the walls of their houses.

SPINNING WOOL INTO THREAD.

FINISHED CLOTH WOUND ROUND BEAM.

SHEARS FOR SHEARING SHEEP – OR CUTTING HAIR!

LOOM →

POSTS LEANED AGAINST WALL.

STONES OR CLAY RINGS TO KEEP THREADS TAUT.

The smith (metalworker) was an important man in Viking society. He may have had a workshop in town or perhaps he was a travelling smith who visited outlying villages and farms. There were always things to be made or mended.

Some smiths were experts at forging sharp swords, other produced delicate jewellery.

CHARCOAL FIRE WITH BELLOWS TO HEAT METAL.

SWORDS WERE MADE BY TWISTING STRANDS OF METAL TOGETHER THEN HAMMERING THEM FLAT. THIS MADE SWORDS STRONG AND FLEXIBLE.

It's beautiful, Erik, but just a little bit heavy.

VIKINGS IN TOWN

Vikings also lived in small villages and small towns. The towns became important trading centres full of craftsmen and merchants.

The buildings were built in much the same way as farmsteads. They were crowded together in narrow streets which must have been very smoky and dirty.

ARAB TRADERS BROUGHT LUXURY ITEMS INTO TOWN LIKE SILK, JEWELLERY, POTTERY, WINE.

A VIKING TOWN

SOME TOWNS WERE PROTECTED
FROM ATTACK BY AN EARTH
RAMPART. WOODEN STOCKADES
WERE BUILT ON THE RAMPART
AND OUT INTO THE SEA.

VIKING FOOD

On their farms, the Vikings grew vegetables and cereals such as oats and barley. They kept all the usual farm animals – cows, sheep, goats, pigs, horses, geese and chickens.

They were able to get other foodstuffs from the wild or from passing merchants.

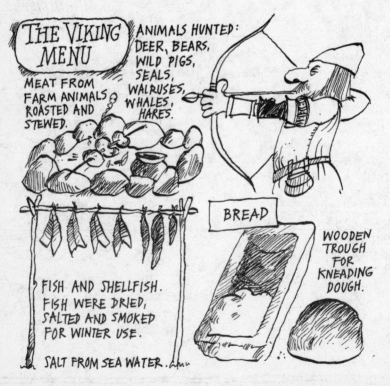

THE VIKING MENU

ANIMALS HUNTED:
DEER, BEARS,
WILD PIGS,
SEALS,
WALRUSES,
WHALES,
HARES.

MEAT FROM FARM ANIMALS ROASTED AND STEWED.

BREAD

WOODEN TROUGH FOR KNEADING DOUGH.

FISH AND SHELLFISH. FISH WERE DRIED, SALTED AND SMOKED FOR WINTER USE.

SALT FROM SEA WATER.

FRUIT FROM THE WILD:
MUSHROOMS, NUTS, BERRIES.

MILK, BUTTER, CHEESE.

HONEY.

BEER MADE FROM
BARLEY AND HOPS.

MEAD MADE FROM
HONEY, WATER AND
YEAST.

WINE AND
SPICES FROM
FOREIGN
TRADERS.

HOME-GROWN
ONIONS, GARLIC,
CABBAGES, LEEKS,
PEAS, APPLES,
HORSERADISH, HERBS.

MEN CLIMBED DOWN
SEA-CLIFFS TO GATHER
EGGS FROM THE
BIRDS NESTING THERE.

VIKING COOKING

Most kitchenware was made of wood except for cauldrons that hung above the fire. Meat was stewed or barbecued above the flames.

Some food was cooked in ovens heated by red-hot stones. Porridge was made from oatmeal or barley.

COW HORNS WERE USED FOR DRINKING FROM. RICH PEOPLE DRANK FROM HORNS DECORATED WITH METALWORK OR GLASS BEAKERS IN THE SHAPE OF HORNS.

SLORP!

BECAUSE OF ITS SHAPE, YOU COULDN'T PUT THE HORN DOWN UNTIL YOU HAD EMPTIED IT!

IRON POT HUNG FROM THE BEAMS.

KNEADING DOUGH.

BREAD BAKED ON FLAT IRON OR STONE.

IRON POT ON TRIPOD WITH HOOKED FEET TO GRIP GROUND.

QUERN FOR GRINDING GRAIN INTO FLOUR. THE GRAIN WAS PUT BETWEEN THE TWO STONES AND THE TOP ONE WAS TURNED WITH A WOODEN HANDLE.

STONES FOR A HEARTH.

VIKING PASTIMES

The Vikings enjoyed their free time. They took part in the same sort of activities we do today. In the summer they swam and had picnics. The men and boys liked to show off their strength and skill in competitions – fencing, archery, rowing, lifting heavy weights, wrestling.

Inside, they sang and danced and played music on pipes or harps. They enjoyed board games.

IN WRESTLING MATCHES, EACH WRESTLER TRIED TO FORCE HIS OPPONENT ON TO THE STONE IN THE MIDDLE OF THE WRESTLING FIELD.

GRUNT!

WHEEZE!

THEY LIKED TO PLACE BETS ON HORSE RACING AND HORSE FIGHTS.

He's a winner!

A MUSICAL PIPE MADE OF BON

Lots of beautifully-carved gaming pieces have been found which belonged to Viking chess sets or board games like Hneftafl – where one player tried to protect his king with eight gaming pieces from attack by the other player who had sixteen gaming pieces.

TOYS CARVED OUT OF WOOD

THE KING FROM AN IVORY CHESS SET.

I told Orm Thinhair not to be too ambitious in the rock-lifting competition.

GETTING AROUND

It was difficult to travel about Scandinavia because of the thick forests, marshes and rugged country. It was easier to travel by boat. However, the Vikings were also expert horse-riders.

In winter they used skis, skates and sledges to get around on the snow and ice.

PUSHING WITH A POLE.

THEY HAD SKATES MADE OF HORSE BONE WHICH THEY CALLED 'ICELEGS'.

WE KNOW THE VIKINGS HAD SKIS AND SNOWSHOES BECAUSE THEY ARE MENTIONED IN THE SAGAS. IT'S POSSIBLE THEY ONLY WORE ONE SKI AND PUSHED THEMSELVES ALONG WITH FOOT AND POLE.

The Vikings often used carts. There were plain ones for transporting goods and decorated ones for carrying rich people. The top part of the cart could be removed and was sometimes used as a coffin. In winter the horses wore spiked shoes called crampons to give them grip on the snow and ice.

THERE WERE VIKING SLEDGES OF ALL SIZES. BIG ONES WERE PULLED BY HORSES. THEY WERE USED ON SNOW AND GRASS.

Bjorn Bluetooth isn't putting much effort into this.

Phew!

VIKING ART

The Vikings loved bright jewellery and ornaments. They put complicated decorations on just about everything – swords, axe-heads, horse-harnesses, helmets, brooches and so on.

Their craftsmen were brilliant at making jewellery from gold, silver, bronze and beads. They were expert at carving in wood and stone.

WHAT THE BEST-DRESSED VIKINGS ARE WEARING

AN ARAB TRADER DESCRIBED VIKING WOMEN AS WEARING 'FINE MAKEUP ON THEIR FACES'.

NECKLACES OF GLASS AND SEMI-PRECIOUS STONES

NECKLACES OF FINELY WOVEN GOLD AND SILVER

ARM RINGS WORN ON THE UPPER ARM WERE POPULAR, AS WERE FINGER RINGS.

ORNATE HELMET DECORATED WITH HUMAN AND ANIMAL FACES.

VIKINGS WHO TRAVELLED TO THE EAST WORE MORE EXOTIC JEWELLERY.

CLOAK PIN AND DECORATED AXE

BROOCHES

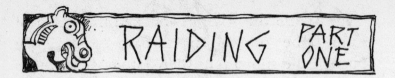

The Vikings began raiding for two reasons. One was wealth. They could carry off lots of good things from a raid on another country – cattle, weapons, slaves, gold, silver and valuable objects.

The other reason was land. Back home the population was getting bigger and there was a shortage of good land for farming. The Vikings began to look around for other places they could set up home.

The Vikings soon had their eyes on England. It was only a short sea-voyage from Scandinavia and there was plenty of good farming land there.

THE ANGLO-SAXONS LIVED IN ENGLAND. LIKE THE VIKINGS, THEY HAD RAIDED THE COUNTRY–BUT SEVERAL CENTURIES BEFORE. THEY DECIDED TO STAY AND THE COUNTRY BECAME ANGLE-LAND.

ANGLE

VIKING

In AD 793 the Vikings attacked the island of Lindisfarne off the north-east coast. They burned the monastery there, stole its treasures and killed some of the monks.

About forty years passed before the next big attack. It was on the island of Sheppey on the River Thames. After that, the Viking attacks became a regular terror for the people living in coastal towns or on riversides.

These people had some relief in winter when the Vikings took their booty home.

In AD 866 a great Viking army arrived in England. It was perhaps made up of about one to two thousand men. This time they had come to stay.

At this time England was divided up into several kingdoms.

Brother Gastric will point out main kingdoms of England.

NORTHUMBRIA

MERCIA

EAST ANGLIA

WESSEX

The Vikings roamed throughout the country, plundering as they went. They stopped during the winter and set up camp. Quite often people paid the Vikings to leave them in peace. This money was called Danegeld (Dane payment).

Eventually, the Vikings had spread themselves over most of the north and the east of the country. Only the kingdom of Wessex in the south held out.

The king of Wessex was Alfred – later known as Alfred the Great. He was an educated man who was interested in books. He ordered monks to keep a historical record of the country. This was called the Anglo-Saxon Chronicle.

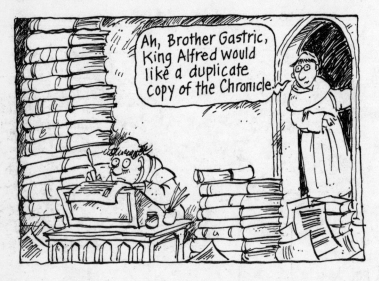

He fortified towns and built warships to try and protect his lands against the constant Viking raids. But in AD 878 a Viking army marched into Wessex under command of their leader Guthrum.

Alfred was defeated and fled into Somerset where he hid in the marshes near Athelney.

He managed to gather another army and defeated the Vikings at the Battle of Edington.

Alfred ordered Guthrum to be baptized as a Christian. The Vikings were to accept Alfred as their overlord and to leave Wessex.

They were allowed to stay in the north and the east. This part of the country became known as the Danelaw as the Vikings were allowed to keep their own laws and customs.

After Alfred died, the kings who ruled England were a mixed bunch – some good, some bad, some awful.

ANGLO-SAXON KINGS – REPORT CARD		
EDWARD THE ELDER	ATHELSTAN	EDMUND
EFFICIENT	BRILLIANT	NOT BAD
EDRED	EADWIG	EDGAR
COULD DO BETTER	TOO YOUNG	EVEN YOUNGER
EDWARD	ETHELRED	EDMUND IRONSIDE
ANOTHER TEENAGER	HOPELESS	AWFUL

The country was not at peace. There were still Viking raids and fighting between the Vikings and Anglo-Saxons.

In AD 1016 a Viking became King of England. His name was Cnut (or Canute) and he was also King of Norway and Denmark. He was considered a wise king and he brought a bit of order to England.

CANUTE WAS THE KING WHO SAT ON HIS THRONE BY THE SEA TO SHOW HIS ADMIRING COURTIERS THAT EVEN A KING COULDN'T COMMAND THE TIDE TO STOP.

See!

In AD 1066 William of Normandy (William the Conqueror) invaded England and became king after the Battle of Hastings. He was a Norman, which was another name for Viking. He was the descendant of Vikings who had settled on the coast of France.

He was a strong king who brought peace to the country and at this point, the Viking raids came to an end.

71

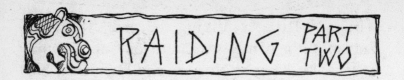

RAIDING PART TWO

The journey from Norway to Shetland was a short one. A Viking ship could do it in twenty-four hours if there was a good wind.

Viking settlers took over Shetland, Orkney, the Hebrides and parts of the Scottish mainland.

The seas round the north and west of Scotland became a regular Viking raiding route. It led to the Isle of Man, north-west England, Ireland and Wales.

The Vikings began to settle in Ireland, and Dublin was their most important trading centre.

A Viking called Sigurd became the first Earl of Orkney and his lands included the islands of the north and west as well as part of the Scottish mainland. Five hundred years would pass before all these lands became part of the kingdom of Scotland.

VIKING WORDS

Quite a few words came into our language from the Vikings. For example: window, egg, die, ski, starboard.

Many more Viking words can be found in place names. By studying the names of villages, farms, and rivers, we can tell where the Vikings settled.

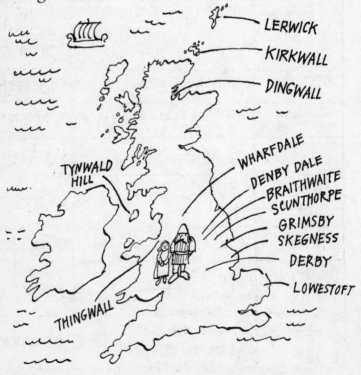

LERWICK

KIRKWALL

DINGWALL

WHARFDALE

DENBY DALE

BRAITHWAITE

SCUNTHORPE

GRIMSBY

SKEGNESS

DERBY

LOWESTOFT

TYNWALD HILL

THINGWALL

SOME BRITISH PLACE NAMES WITH VIKING CONNECTIONS		
VIKING WORD	MEANING	PLACE
THING + VOLLR	(THE VIKING ASSEMBLY) THERE ARE NAMES ALL OVER THE COUNTRY WHICH MEAN 'THE PLACE WHERE THE THING MET'. OPEN SPACE	DINGWALL (SCOTLAND) TYNWALD HILL (ISLE OF MAN) THINGWALL (ENGLAND)
BY	A FARMSTEAD	DERBY DENBY GRIMSBY
TOFT	A HOMESTEAD	LOWESTOFT
THORPE	AN OUTLYING FARM	SCUNTHORPE
NESS	A HEADLAND	SKEGNESS
HVARF DALE	BEND VALLEY	WHARFDALE
THVEIT	A MEADOW OR CLEARING	BRAITHWAITE
KIRK VAGR	CHURCH BAY	KIRKWALL
LEIK VIK	MUD BAY OR CREEK	LERWICK

VIKING BURIAL

The Vikings believed in life after death so when they died, they were buried with some of their possessions that they might need in their next life.

Slaves and poor people had very little in their graves, but the graves of rich people were crammed with things. This sometimes included slaves who agreed to be killed so they could go to the next life with their owners.

SOME EXAMPLES OF THINGS FOUND IN VIKING GRAVES

A POOR MAN OR SLAVE	A SINGLE KNIFE.
A HOUSEWIFE	MILK PAIL, SEWING AND WEAVING EQUIPMENT.
A MERCHANT	SCALES, PIECES OF SILVER.
A CHIEFTAIN OR HIS WIFE	LAID IN FUNERAL SHIP (FULL SIZE) DRESSED IN FINE CLOTHES. SWORDS AND OTHER WEAPONS, JEWELLERY, FURNITURE, HORSES, CARTS, DOGS. EXOTIC ITEMS, FOR INSTANCE: PEACOCKS, PRECIOUS ORNAMENTS FROM ABROAD. THE CHIEFTAIN'S SLAVES WERE SOMETIMES KILLED AND BURIED WITH THEIR MASTER.

Sometimes the funeral ships of rich people were set alight and burned; sometimes they were buried.

RELATIVES OF THE DEAD PERSON LIT THE FIREWOOD ROUND THE SHIP.

AN OLD WOMAN WAS USUALLY IN CHARGE OF THE PREPARATIONS. SHE WAS KNOWN AS THE 'ANGEL OF DEATH'.

THE ASHES OF THE SHIP WERE COVERED AND A POLE WAS STUCK ON THE MOUND WITH THE DEAD PERSON'S NAME ON IT.

Graves were marked by a mound, pole or stone. Sometimes stones were laid round the grave in the shape of a boat.

GOOD PEOPLE WENT TO SPEND THEIR NEXT LIFE IN THE HEAVENLY COUNTRY OF ASGARD. (FOOD AND DRINK WERE SOMETIMES BURIED WITH THE DEAD AS REFRESHMENT ON THEIR JOURNEY THERE.)

IN ASGARD THEY SPENT THEIR TIME HOBNOBBING WITH THE GODS.

NOT SO GOOD PEOPLE ENDED UP IN THE LAND OF THE DEAD. A BEAUTIFUL WOMAN CALLED HEL WAS IN CHARGE THERE. – BUT ONLY HER TOP HALF WAS BEAUTIFUL – THE BOTTOM HALF WAS A SKELETON! SHE WAS SISTER TO A SERPENT AND A WOLF.

FARM-WORKERS WERE BURIED NEAR THEIR FARMS TO BRING GOOD LUCK.

Oh no! Not grandad here again!

Boo!

HOW DO WE KNOW ABOUT VIKINGS?

Although the Vikings didn't write down much about themselves, we know a lot about them.

THE FOREIGNER'S VIEW

...and I'll tell you another thing...

Foreign merchants and travellers who had dealings with the Vikings left descriptions of them and their customs.

THE MONK'S VIEW

Monks were among the few people who could write in those times. They wrote down a lot about the Viking raids as well as their poems and sagas.

THE CHRISTIAN MONKS DIDN'T THINK MUCH OF THE PAGAN VIKINGS!

THE THROWN-AWAY THINGS

Treasured items such as swords or jewellery were often thrown into marshes and rivers as a gift to the gods.

What an odd-shaped trout!

THE BURIED THINGS   HOARDS

Vikings sometimes buried their valuables in times of danger. These hoards are occasionally discovered. Perhaps their owners had been killed or forgot where their treasures had been buried.

But I'm sure I buried it next to the gnarled tree, thirty paces south from the stone that looks like a rabbit!

We can learn a lot from the things found buried in Viking graves.

Materials such as clothing, leather and wood usually rot away but sometimes they are preserved if they are underwater or in boggy ground.

The ship graves of rich chieftains and their wives provide lots of objects and clues about Vikings.

WHALEBONE SMOOTHING BOARD FOR SMOOTHING CLOTH. (PERHAPS!)

BEDPOST WITH CARVED ANIMAL'S HEAD WITH A CURLY TONGUE.

BRONZE KEY.

DECORATED DRINKS BUCKET FROM A LADY'S GRAVE.

SMALL SILVER STATUE OF A GOD HOLDING WEAPONS.

Archaeologists have the job of finding these things.

Sometimes they find small things like pieces of silver or an axe head.

Sometimes they find large and important things . . .

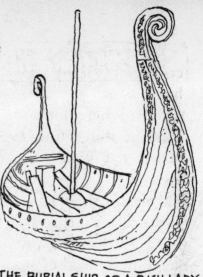

THE BURIAL SHIP OF A RICH LADY. MANY OBJECTS WERE FOUND IN THE SHIP INCLUDING A DECORATIVE CART AND SLEDGE. EVEN SOME PLANTS HAD SURVIVED.

. . . like the Oseberg ship found in Norway . . .

. . . or the Viking houses found at York . . .

SHOE, COMB AND PAN PIPES.

. . . or the Viking farmstead discovered at Jarlshof in Shetland.

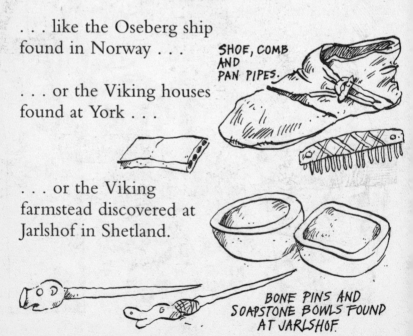

BONE PINS AND SOAPSTONE BOWLS FOUND AT JARLSHOF.

Whether they were raiding or trading, the colourful Vikings have made their mark on history!